in
Wors
yoga,

365 Prayers to the Angels

*Get you prayers answered
and fulfill all your dreams
with the help of the Angels.*

HUMAN ANGELS

Copyright © 2019 Human Angels
All rights reserved.

Introduction

Do you need a new job? Need to increase your financial wealth? Want to meet your life partner? Have to solve health problems? Know how to release old emotional wounds?

Call the angels, pray to them. Your wishes and dreams are immediately fulfilled as soon as you realize the power of teaming with your Angels. Nothing is impossible for them to handle.

This book helps you make the act of praying to your Angels become an essential part of your daily life. Once you decide to open your heart to the Angels your life becomes happier and easier. Amazing things start to happen, synchronicity manifests in many forms, unexpected opportunities that you could not see or imagine open up before your eyes. Obstacles and difficulties that you have long been struggling with spontaneously fade away.

In the rush of your life, these angelic prayers will be your precious inner space of peace and light. They will be your secret source of strength and inspiration for a better life. It's time to stop feeling powerless, complaining about misfortune. Recruit legions of Angels at your beck and call to obtain success at work, in relationships, and in society. Just be ready to ask and open to receive. All you need to do to invoke the Angels at your side and to pray to them. Let these prayers become your daily instruments to connect with your Angels. They will bring love, happiness, wealth, health, and good luck into your life.

The Angels are just waiting for you to invite them into your world. You have to call and pray to them because Angels cannot intervene in your life unless you ask them to do so. They respect your free will. In fact, the sacred law of free will doesn't allow them to intervene in your life without your permission. Remember that every time you ask for help, an Angel fulfils their purpose. The immediate help of angels is available to you at any time and at any place. Invite and welcome them into your life.

How can the Angels help you in a practical way.

Here are some examples:

• The Angels can help you make contact with the right people you need to meet at a perfect time: a new partner, new friends, more customers for your business, good advice to invest your money, personal referral to get you a new and better job,…

• The Angels can provide you with the resources you need to fulfil your practical needs: financial support, supplies, education, wealth for your family, the perfect spot for your new house,…

- The Angels can give you strength when you feel overwhelmed and help you to stay calm when everything around you is a mess.

The Angels help you to make wise decisions, to stay positive in difficult times, and they also help you to achieve a higher self-love and self-respect. Everyone around you will acknowledge you for who you are: a divine being full of positive resources. All you have to do is to start praying to your Angels and let them help you.

Your prayers will put Angels at work and nothing makes an Angel happier than to help you. Every time you ask for help, an Angel fulfils its mission, and you achieve your goals and live a miraculous life!

The 7 Golden Rules to make your prayers work amazingly

1. Focus on heart centered breathing

Relax, make yourself comfortable and make sure that when you start your prayer you will not be disturbed. After taking a few relaxing breaths, bring your awareness to your heart and start to breathe for a few seconds a little more deeply than usual. As you breathe in, imagine you are doing so through your heart and, as you breathe out, imagine doing so through your heart. Imagine to breathe in and breathe out love and light. As you start to breathe deeply, you can also place your hands over your heart to be better focused on your heart-centered breathing. In this way, you raise your vibration and you begin to tune in to the angelic realms. Being aware of your heart power and connecting with the highest vibrations of love are the keys to communicate with your Angels. Angels speak the language of the heart, they do everything for love, and they respond with love. Angels are able to hear your heartfelt plea, and so if you are sincere in your request they will hear you and get the message to step in and help.

2. Read your prayer

When your heart is open, the angelic realm becomes accessible to you. Now you can open the book and pick up your prayer. You can open it randomly or, if you prefer, you can simply read the prayers in the order of the book. Focus only on the prayer you choose as if the outer world does not exist. If the circumstance allows you, read it out loud. If you cannot do this, just say the prayer silently, simply moving your lips. If there is any thought crossing your head, let it go and focus back on your heart and on your prayer.

While you pray, you may feel a gentle breeze flowing across the room or a light touch on your shoulder. You might also feel chills or goosebumps as the confirmation that your Angels are there. These signs are the Angels' way of telling you that they are with you and that they are listening to your prayer.

3. Set powerful intentions

When you pray, set powerful intentions. What does 'intention' mean? Intention is the energy that you attach to your prayer. Say, visualize, feel the words of the prayer. The heart is the fuel that empowers your prayers with its intentions. There is a great power in setting intentions and creating a designated direction through words. Intentions state your willingness and openness to receive. A powerful intention is the best way to declare to the Angels that you are ready to receive.

4. Visualize Angels and hand everything over to them

During your time of invocation and prayer, imagine that the angels are all around you and present with you, wherever you are at the moment of your prayer. When you visualize Angels around you, you're effectively calling them into your presence. Then release all expectations of how your request will be answered by them.

5. Use this secret 'weapon' to empower your prayer

The positive outcome of your prayers to the Angels will increase dramatically when you start to use this secret 'weapon', the power of colors. Learning how to use the power of colors in your prayers will allow you to achieve your goals without effort and be successful. The Angels are beings of light and, as you certainly know, light fractionates into 7 colors. The order of colors in light is called the visible spectrum of light. It runs from violet to red. The same 'law' applies to Angels. The metaphysical system of the Angels' colors is based on seven different light rays made of seven different colors. Every color brings a specific kind of vibration and energy (protection, healing, wisdom, ...). Angels respond to the chromatic vibration that springs from the energy of a single color. Every Angel, in fact, can help you in a specific way and only serves a specific colored ray. Because of this, it becomes extremely helpful to visualize the colors when you're asking for help from your Angels. When you pray, visualize the color which carries the essential quality of the Angels you would like to attract. The vibrational essence of your chosen color brings you immediately in alignment with the angelic help you seek.

Here are the colors and their energies:

VIOLET Energy of spiritual wisdom

BLUE Energy of protection

GREEN Energy of healing and prosperity

PINK Energy of love and peace

YELLOW Energy of wisdom for decisions

ORANGE Energy of well being and optimism

RED Energy of strength and power

For example, if you're feeling sick… Read your prayer and, in the meantime, visualize a green light and Angels all around you pouring Divine love into your presence. For example, if you're worried about a family member, imagine them wrapped in a orange light, in a happy, positive state with Angels all around them helping to create blessings in their lives.

In order to help your concentration on one specific color, you can also surround yourself with objects (clothing, accessories, foods, crystals,...) of similar colour with the type of angelic assistance you would like to receive.

For example. You don't know what to do. You have received a job offer and you don't know whether to accept it or keep the old job. While you pray to receive clarity you can wear a yellow scarf and wearing it for the rest of the day will help you stay focused on your request.

There is also another effective way to connect with the specific angelic energy of which you are in need: lighting a colored candle. When you use a colored candle to pray to your Angels you immediately relate to the Angels in charge of your request. Lightening a candle for a particular purpose or intention is practiced worldwide. Lighting a candle symbolizes bringing the light of faith to our wishes or desires.

6. Imagine that your prayer has already been answered

Remember this: every prayer is being listened to, at any time, by your Angels. Every prayer is answered and Grace is always granted. You are unconditionally loved by Angels.

Imagine that your desire has come true. Do not focus on 'how' it has happened, but only on the fact that it 'has happened'. Imagine what you would like to achieve in your life, then start to feel as if you had already achieved it. In a prayer, what always matters is the feeling of being and of having what you wish for. Imagine, for example, that you wish help from your Angels in manifesting a new job. You'll have to be in fine tune with the essence of what you want and 'see' yourself in your new job. You need to dive deep into the vibes and feelings of having what you want to create. When you set an intention with a mindset of openness to receive, you affirm that what you are seeking is already being provided, is already created and made available for your use. As you learn to clear out blocks, patterns, and karmic connections that no longer serve you, you are better able to receive your heart's desires. You start to see that all is in Divine Order and you can relax more into acceptance of what flows in your life.

7. *Be Grateful*

To thank the Angels is really important, but not for them, because giving is their true nature. They give for the pure joy of giving. To thank them is important for you because gratitude always brings more blessings. The feeling of gratitude is like a signal that you send to the Universe showing that you are open to receive. It's like a powerful magnet that attracts complementary energies into your life. This is why you have to send your gratitude to the Angels even though they have no need for thanks.

365

Prayers to the Angels

Thank you for your presence and guidance that inspire me to work as an earth angel helping, blessing and uplifting others.

Please, guide me to embody the light and presence of the Divine into my life. Make my life a sacred path of love where my heart and soul blossom. Please, inspire my life journey so that my footsteps may be of benefit to others.

Please, whatever happens in my life and in the world, guide me to never be discouraged and always keep my trust in the power of good to overcome evil and the power of love to overcome hatred.

Please, fill my being with the power to dream without letting self-judgment, self-limitations, or a sense of worthlessness poison my dreams.

Please, enable me to say goodbye to the toxic relationships in my life; to anyone who puts me down with words or actions, who makes me invisible, who blackmails me emotionally. Please, help me say a loving and compassionate goodbye to all of them and guide me to new happy loving relationships based on mutual love, trust and respect.

Please, help me release fears, doubts and restrictive beliefs so that I may embody the spiritual power within me. Purify me so that I may let the light of the Divine shine in my life and through my life. Cleanse me from any self-limitation and make me a generous and powerful miracle worker.

I give you heartfelt thanks for all the love and goodness you show me. Thank you for blessing my world. Thank you for assisting me with such patient loyalty. Thank you for wrapping me in your protective wings and making me feel safe and loved in your angelic presence.

Please, remind me not to rush through life with an anxious mind. Help me wake up with a relaxed and confident attitude, put a smile on my face and keep it smiling until the end of the day.

Please, guide me in removing any hindrance that may interfere with the divine flow of abundance. Make me open to receive the gift of financial wealth and riches. I ask you to remove my anxieties, fears and worries about money, and replace them with the awareness that prosperity is my natural state of being. Let me allow money to come into my life easily, abundantly and effortlessly.

When I am tempted to judge others as a way of feeling above them or as a way of making me feel better about myself, please, guide me to practice a non-judgmental mindfulness and love others with an unconditional heart.

Please, help me forgive the people who have spoken against me and tried to harm me. Remind me to pray for them and transmit love and compassion so that their negativity will no longer affect me.

When I feel lost, please, hold me tight in your arms, so that I can be stronger than all the fears and all the challenges in my life.

Please, help me not to sabotage myself and to recognize when my thoughts are in direct conflict with my happiness. Guide me to release every self-defeating attitude that stands in the way of my own happiness.

Please, bless my house, cleanse it from negative influences of any kind and allow only good to enter. Grant me your protection so that my home may always be filled with positivity, peace and waves of laughter.

Please, help my loved ones that have passed away to have a smooth and peaceful transition back home to heaven. Help me remember them with love and gratitude rather than with pain and despair. Please, fill my void and heal my grief.

When despair and confusion reign within me, please, calm my anxious spirit. Grant me patience and confidence. Help me remember that everything is always in divine order so that I have nothing to fear or worry about.

Please, help me understand my own needs and limitations. Give me guidance to set healthy boundaries for my own wellness. Help me be there for others but never leave myself behind.

Each time a problem arises, please, allow me not to worry and to rely on your help. Remind me that you are always by my side, assisting me until the problem is resolved, and not allowing anything to disturb my peace of mind or inner tranquility.

Please, help me not to take myself too seriously. Please remind me to laugh often and heartily.

Please, cheer me up when I am down, give me confidence in the face of uncertainty and joy in the face of suffering. Help me find myself when I feel lost. Let me discover my true sense and reinvent my happy self, moment by moment.

Please, guide me to bring my truth to others from a loving place. Remind me that I cannot force anyone to comprehend a message that they are not yet ready to receive. But nevertheless help me to never underestimate the power of planting a seed.

Please, help me let go of any resentment. Help me remember that in the innocence of my heart everything is already forgiven.

Please, help me remove all the negative feelings and thoughts that make me think and act as a victim. Every time I fall into the pitfalls of this mental attitude, remind me of the powerful, divine being that I am.

Please, help me live in the present. Help me release doubts and fears, and ground me into the present moment. Keep me aligned to the "now", aware and attentive so that I may seize the blessing of every moment.

When I am doubtful, please guide my actions. Help me to know when to leave and when to stay, when to surrender and when to struggle, when to let go and when to hold on. Please, point me in the right direction at any crossway on my path of life.

Please, help me live in accordance to my highest potential and bring me closer to my soul's purpose. Help me uncover my heavenly assignment where joy and fulfillment lie.

Please, awaken me in body and spirit each day with a desire to be better than the day before.

Teach me to connect with your presence and insights in my dreams. Tune me to the messages that you bring forth while I sleep. Help me be able to use the guidance you provide me through my dreams to overcome challenges, solve problems. Protect myself and my family from danger, unveil the future, and open me up to unlimited new opportunities. Please, fill my dreams with your guidance and help me to make it part of my daily life.

When my heart feels lonely and my soul has lost courage, please, whisper in my ear that I am always loved and worthy of the best. Surround me with comfort and ease. Shower me with blessings and flood my path with your glowing light.

Please, pour your grace over me today and may I, in turn, share my grace with others.

Please, remind me that I have all I need within me. Help me remember that is my divine birthright to manifest a joyous, successful and abundant life.

I give you immense thanks for inspiring me, for being my peaceful oasis of grace in a world of chaos and turmoil. Thank you for helping me stay balanced and wise in this frantic world.

Please, give me the courage to step out of my comfort zone. Help me not to remain within the boundaries of where I feel comfortable and be able to face the fear of venturing beyond them.

Every day, stand guard at the door of my heart. Please, shield it from resentment, anger, greed, deceit, envy, pride, jealousy and any other low-frequency emotion. Purify, protect and uplift my heart so that it may always be aligned to the high frequencies of your loving light.

Please, open my life to the limitless potential of my spiritual gifts and guide me to put them to the service of others. Inspire me to truly live my divine purpose so that I may awaken the light within me and the power of committed love in action.

Please, open my heart, uplift my spirit, clear my mind, and make a wider place for love and compassion in me.

Please, help me attract like-minded people so that we can work together and put the different gifts each of us has to offer to service of the greater good.

Please, help me always remember how blessed I am. Inspire me to express my thankful heart in prayer and returned acts of kindness.

Please, guide me not to fall into the pitfalls of jealousy. Make me aware that jealousy is routed into my sense of self-unworthiness and built upon my insecurities. Make me aware that it is nothing but love gone wrong through fear. Please, help me release, heal and transform my jealousy into confidence and trust.

Please, protect my family and I from any negativity, seen or unseen. Cancel all negative thoughts and actions directed at me or any member of my family. Shield us with your light and keep negativity away. Guard us now and always in the shelter of your love.

Please, enable me to bring the blessing of your angelic light into this troubled world. Let me spread your divine glow continually so that to shine and radiate love may become my natural state of being.

Please, give me guidance so that I may embrace every problem that comes my way as a meaningful lesson, rather than an annoying and senseless inconvenience. Help me treasure your guidance so that I may learn quickly from every life lesson with a flexible mind and an open heart.

Please, help me say "no" to things that are unimportant and that do nothing more than consume my time. Inspire me to invest my energies and time wisely in people and things that align with my highest purpose.

Please, motivate me when I feel weak and give me the courage to never give up. Give me the strength not to throw in the towel and to conquer my goals. Help me do it for myself, for my loved ones and for all the people who can be inspired by me.

Please, inspire me to develop true self-confidence and no longer need other people to accept me or tell me how good I am. Inspire me with unconditional self-acceptance so that I may be fully satisfied and fulfilled with how I am.

Every time I fall, please, lend me your merciful hand to get on my feet. Every time I fall, please, give me your help, and give me the faith and the power to be stronger than before.

Please, teach me how to love more and more. Replenish my cells, my mind, my heart with love so that I may become a manifestation and an embodiment of love.

Please, make me aware when I try, with judgment, projections or expectations to disconnect from what the present moment brings to me. Give me the wisdom to stay deeply rooted in the "here and now" so that I may be open to the infinite possibilities of the present moment.

Please, help me become sovereign and responsible for my own life instead of fearing external conditions and circumstances. Release old energy patterns so that I may totally express the powerful creator and divine being that I am.

Please, help me be content in the midst of whatever situation or circumstance I find myself. Breathe contentment into my heart so that I may feel the beauty and the magic of life at any given moment.

Please, help me be aligned with divine well-being and infinite abundance and always believe in my abilities to attract a prosperous life.

Please, inspire me to find peace within myself and merge with it so that I may spread peace upon the earth wherever I go.

When obstacles arise, please, help me practice perseverance and patience. Help me never give up and go on, despite any difficulty or delay, so that I may stay true to my desired course.

Please, help me to heal my family's karma. Free me from it manifesting itself in the form of self-destructive tendencies and repetitive patterns of behaviour. Give me guidance so that I may release my karma in all directions of time, in this or any other life, for the past and future generations and for every member of my present family.

Please, assist me during any difficult times and remind me that they are only a temporary shadow in an eternal world of light.

Please, instruct me to think before I speak. When I am about to say negative, hurtful or disparaging words to someone, please set a guard over my lips before words rush out of them. Guide me to remain silent or only speak up from a place of love and understanding.

Please, help me make those around me feel loved. Give me the openness to show them how much they matter to me. Remind me always to acknowledge their presence and efforts, and never take them for granted. Enable me to show how blessed I am to have them in my life.

Please, dissolve any sense of separation and teach me the true transformative power of unconditional love. Inspire me to bring love to the world around me rather than expecting love from it. Make unconditional love my way of life.

Please, clear my heart from feeling guilty. Help me see my past actions not as mistakes but as a way to learn and grow. Grant me your guidance so that I may transform my brokenness into a blessing and move forward with a healed and grateful heart.

Please, remind me that every person that comes into my life comes for a reason. Remind me that everybody is meaningful in my life so that, with humility, I may always learn something from everyone and grow into the fullness of my being.

Please, help me be strong, brave and capable of taking care of those I love during difficult times. Give me guidance so that I may be able to hold their hands and walk with them through their tough moments. Please, help me be an angel to them.

Please, help me believe in a world free of all inequity, violence, hatred, discrimination, intolerance and racism. Help me commit myself to do everything possible to eliminate the root causes of every injustice. Guide me to devote my life to the task of being an instrument of justice, peace, fairness and universal brotherhood.

Please, inspire me to be kind to others, have a compassionate heart and spread love everywhere I go. Help me pass on, multiplied, all the love that I receive from you.

Please, help me honour my inner child and always be in touch with its qualities of spontaneity, creativity and joy. Guide me to live with a cheerful heart, be wildly enthusiastic about life and allow my inner child to come out and play.

Please, give me the awareness that I cannot change my past or undo my mistakes. Help me stop judging and condemning myself because of them. Please, help me forgive myself, now and forever.

I pray for your help with my loved ones, family and friends that are dealing with physical issues. Hold them in your loving arms. Fill their bodies, from the top of their heads to the soles of their feet, with your healing light and make their hearts overflow with strength and hope.

Please, make your spiritual guidance clear. Help me not only hear and fully understand it but also speak it, share it with others and comprehend the miraculous power of your words of wisdom to change my life and that of those around me.

Please, help me keep myself in check and make me able to recognize when I am pretending, manipulating, concealing or lying. Inspire me to always be righteous so that I may stay true to my integrity and let my potential grow into enlightened relationships with others.

Please, remind me that nothing is going to happen to me today or any other day of my life that you and I can't handle together.

Please, help me celebrate my wins no matter how big or small. Infuse me with a sense of contentment so that I may relax and give up my stressful search for perfection. Guide me to be lenient with myself, give myself a pat on the back and be proud of what I have already achieved.

Please, guide me to be patient and give thanks in the midst of adversity, by remembering that nothing happens to me but everything happens for me.

Please, grant me compassion so that I may always be in a never-ending state of loving and non-judgemental understanding towards everyone.

Please, give me the confidence to never give up on my dreams even when nobody else but me believes they can come true. Lead me towards the fulfilment of my abundant and wildest dreams. Lead me towards the most epic life.

Please, grant me clarity of thought. Help me distinguish between good and evil, fair and unfair, right and wrong within every situation. Please, bless me with the gift of discernment and guide my footsteps so that I may always walk righteously and stay true to my path of light.

Please, help me be a balanced person. Let me discover a sense of stability in who I am. Give me a mindset that has harmony and constancy in its movement. Please, attune and harmonize me with your angelic grace.

Please, erase my doubts about my power to manifest my dreams. Improve my manifestation abilities and transform me from a greenhorn to a powerful and successful manifestor.

Please, help me realize that my worth as a person is not dependent on being accepted or valued by others. Free me from the need to look outside myself to confirm my worthiness. Inspire me to be the loving center of my life.

Please, help me never to let my pride get in the way of my relationships. Help me listen to others with an open spirit rather than an 'I know it all' attitude. Please, inspire me to live with simplicity and humbleness of heart.

Please, stay on guard around me to protect my family, my pets and myself. Surround all of us with your loving care and remove negative forces. Don't allow any energy to enter my house, my neighborhood and my workplace for intentions that are other than love.

Please, bless my relationships and make them strong and healthy. Give me guidance to balance them with harmony and peace. Please, shower my relationships with the blessings of patience, loyalty, respect, kindness and understanding.

Please, help me overcome my relationship issues. Give me the wisdom to be grateful to the people with whom I have problematic relationships because, through them, I can recognize those parts of myself that need to be accepted, harmonized and healed. Those parts of myself that, with your help, I now invite into the wholeness of my being.

Please, awaken me in body and spirit each day with the desire to improve myself. Inspire me to become the best version of myself. Give me your guidance so that, by making myself better, I may make the world a better place.

Please, help me not to judge but see the divine perfection that is hidden in every moment of life. Help me see the perfection of the whole world beyond its apparent imperfection.

Please, guide me to focus my actions on obtaining success beyond all my self-limitations. Help me create wealth and abundance in alignment with my soul mission, and manifest the kind of success that serves myself and humanity for the highest good.

Whatever occurs to me or around me, please grant me the wisdom to remember that nothing ever happens by chance: everything happens for a reason and always in perfect divine timing. Guide me to be at peace with all that has happened, is happening and will happen.

Please, help me love myself the way I am. Guide me to love myself as you love me: unconditionally, boundlessly and wholeheartedly.

When a new challenge unexpectedly comes up in my life, please, infuse me with the power of acceptance. Guide me to embrace everything that occurs in my life with a confident and fearless heart.

Please, help me stop seeing my life as a struggle where I am constantly battling it out. Help me surrender with confidence to the flow of life, stand by and watch everything fall effortlessly into place.

Please, inspire me to work for the greater good. Inspire me to give kindness and care wherever needed. Inspire me to do what has to be done for the benefit of all mankind.

Please, cleanse my home. Spread your light in every corner of it and cast away any negative energy so it may always be my peaceful dwelling place and safe haven.

Every time I meet someone, please, remind me to focus on what I appreciate in them so that I can see them glowing. Please, guide me to look at everyone as if they already radiate their divine potential.

Please, show me the lesson hidden within every happening. Help me understand, easily and effortlessly, all my soul lessons during this lifetime so that I may grow quickly, move forward and leave the past in the past.

Please, infuse me with your blessed light, so I may feel restored to full well-being. Renew, regenerate and recharge all the cells in my body. Pour peace, love and bliss through my veins. Embrace me and make me feel joyfully healthy.

Thank you for holding my hand when I am fighting fear and despairing. Thank you for walking with me and for not leaving me to fend for myself. Thank you for illuminating my path and being by my side when I need it most. Thank you for banishing the shadows of my faithlessness and allow your angelic light to shine through me.

Please, relieve the pain caused by the death of my loved ones. Help me regain peace and joy in the knowledge that their souls sweetly rest in the arms of heaven's angels. Please, let them know that they are infinitely loved and shine my endless love upon their souls. Help me open a divine connection with my loved ones, that death can never erase nor decrease.

Please, inspire me to fully witness my inner light. If I come into contact with darkness, help me keep on shining and never allow darkness to become a part of me. Guide me to be a glowing beacon that spreads love.

Please, help me purify my spirit by releasing and dissolving any negative feelings toward myself and others. Return me to the original innocence of my spotless soul.

When I feel anger and I am about to react in a bad way, please hold your hand over my head, help me breathe deeply, calm down and take a step back. Help me return to a state of love, forgiveness and understanding.

Please, give me guidance so that I may make choices that are for the good of everyone. Guide me to be mindful so that I may always know the best decisions to make and always do the right thing, however great the cost appears to be.

Please, infuse me with the power of silence so that I may move on from all the noise of the world, and regain a state of inner balance and deep stillness. Enable me to relish the joys of silence so that I may listen to the deep inner voice of my soul. Guide me to attain the spiritual peace that comes from being perfectly at one with my own true self.

Please, make me a light for others so they can be guided in times of darkness. Give me guidance so that I may hold their hands in their most hopeless moments and help them find the way to their hearts.

Please, give me the courage to speak up and speak the truth. Guide me to speak up for the voiceless, the weak, the needy and the oppressed. Infuse me with the will to stand up for what I believe, even if it means standing alone.

Please, bless me with a new sense of self-worth and self-acceptance so that I may acknowledge my strength and accept my vulnerability. Help me to be ok with myself and love who I am in the way I am. No matter what.

Please, teach me how to love my family and friends unconditionally, and how to change all my relationships that need help in the most positive and loving ways. Improve all my connections and fill me with an enlivening and peaceful sense of connectedness to all life.

Thank you for clearing away my insecurity and fear, and showing me that I am a ray of divine light here to enlighten this world, be happy and give joy to everyone who crosses my path.

Please, guide me to release what is holding me back from enjoying my life fully. Help me release anything that is blocking me from experiencing the blessing present in every moment of life.

Please, help me be mindful of what I eat and drink. Guide me to respect, honour, care, cherish and love my body. Help me give my body the nourishment, exercise, rest and comfort it needs so that it may always be perfectly healthy.

Please, enable me to deal with my emotional reactivity and guide me not to act in a way that I might regret. Teach me not to react badly and to replace defensiveness and animosity with understanding. Guide me to stop behaving in hurtful ways and not to take action until I am able to act through the heart and respond with love.

Please, strengthen me so that I may overcome insecurity and low self-esteem that I face every time I decide to step outside of my comfort zone and dare to be different. Help me to spread the wings of my imagination wide and let my mind soar confidently. Give me guidance to not just dream about becoming great but take action to make it happen.

Please, help me when I am tempted to throw in the towel, when I am tired of believing for a miracle. Fill me with the strength to go on even when I feel like I can't take another step. With your help I'll never give up.

I give you immense thanks for gently delving into my heart and listen to my prayer even when it is silent, even when is unknown to my own conscience.

Please, help me overcome my impatience. Shower my relationships with the blessing of patience and let me reflect your serenity and peacefulness.

I ask for your spiritual healing energy to flow through every cell of my body restoring it to health and wholeness. Please, infuse me with your beautiful and powerful light so I may always feel vibrantly healthy.

Please, help me tap into the wondrous manifestation powers that are hidden within myself. Teach me how to harness and use them to achieve what I want and become the mighty master of my own destiny.

I thank you for your guidance that makes me able to discern what is best in each and every situation. I thank you for the divine guidance you give me each day so that I can grow in love, grace and service.

Please, teach me all I need to know about respect. Teach me to respect others in their choices and demand that they respect mine. Please, instruct me so that I may prevent anyone from violating the sacredness of my self-respect.

Please, help me be good and kind to myself. Help me practice self-love so that I may live a life that truly shines.

Please, give me your graceful help to instantly heal all the sources of my emotional pain. Remove all my unhealed hurts. Bring your restoring light to all the emotions that have caused me feelings of sadness, loneliness and despair so that I may bear witness to your healing power.

Please, help me let go of mental constraints so that I may achieve an expanded state of being. Shift my energetic field so that I may vibrate higher. Attune me to your angelic light and enable me to embody, hold and share your glowing energy.

Please, teach me to be humbly proud. Please, teach me how to respect all people, but grovel to none.

Please, grant me clarity of purpose and strengthen my will so that I may consciously walk into the dimension of love that I have always belonged to and be the light that I have always been.

Please, help me maintain a devoted attitude towards Mother Earth, endangered from all sides nowadays. Guide me to live my life in gratitude to her and her abundant gifts. Inspire me to contribute to protecting the delicate and precious web of life on planet earth.

Please, help me have eyes to see the best in others, a peaceful mind to forgive them, a generous heart to offer words of encouragement and loving support in any way possible.

Please, help me be mindful of everyone and have mercy on them while remembering that everyone is carrying an invisible burden and everyone is struggling with their own, silent battle.

Please, help me not be weighed down by the negativity of the world. Fill me with your purifying light so that I may wash away, release and transmute any dense vibrational energy. Please, lift me up to embody my divine, angelic self.

Please, help me release the illusion of directing the flow of life and all my false convictions about how life should be. Teach me how not to be in control, surrender to your loving guidance and confidently hand over the reins of my life to you.

Please, guide me to be selfless and help everyone in their hour of need, without expecting anything in return. Guide me to be of service to others with no expectations of reward or recognition. Help me always keep in mind that giving is already receiving.

Please, help me constantly monitor my thoughts and clear them from any self-limiting belief. Give me guidance so that I may release every thought pattern related to scarcity and limitation that causes me to attract a lack-based reality. Guide me to effortlessly manifest my desired life.

Please, make the love I have for myself so strong that I may never again deny myself or sabotage my happiness. Help me choose to love myself by choosing not to stand in the way of my own happiness.

Please, help me not look back but move forward. Make me flexible and open to change. Make me ready to let go of the life I had planned and let the signs show me the way so that I may confidently follow the ever-surprising path of my heart.

Please, help me stop finding excuses not to be happy. Help me stop waiting for others to make me content. Give me guidance so that I may tap into my inner, endless and always present source of happiness.

When I fail, please, console me, cheer me up and help me remember that failure doesn't mean I should give up; it means I must try harder. Help me keep in mind that failing doesn't mean I am a loser; it is just a step on the path to my self-realization.

Please, teach me how to use my money with intelligence, self-control and discipline to prepare the best future for myself and all concerned.

Please, help my actions stem from a place of love rather than from a place of imbalance. Inspire me to be a loving presence everywhere I go. Give me guidance so that I may sow and reap love.

Thank you for encouraging me when I am disheartened and for instructing me when I err in judgment. Thank you for making me feel safe and protected in your loving presence. Thank you for providing me with the strength I need. Thank you for your continuous assistance and your endless supply of blessings.

Into your hands I release my anger, I surrender my resentment, I let go of my bitterness. Please, clear and erase every toxic emotion every time they try to return to me.

Please, inspire me to radiate goodness. Let graciousness, integrity, humbleness, compassion, unity and peacefulness follow me wherever I go. Inspire me to do righteous things that positively unfold in order to bring myself and humanity closer to the alignment with Divine Love and wisdom.

Please, help me always behave in ways that are in accordance with my personal values and never betray them, and through them, betray myself.

Please, help me be wise enough to only seek relationships that bring me positivity at all levels. Give me the strength to let go of any relationship that holds me back or is no longer for my highest and best good.

Please, banish negative thoughts and stop them from rolling perpetually through my mind. Help me interrupt the flow of my thoughts and break free from my inner noise. Please, help me let the silence unfold its peaceful and gentle power over me.

Please, help me remember you through the busy rush of life. Help me never forget that you are walking with me at any given moment, inspiring me to share my gift of love and joy with others.

Please, shine your light upon my family. Give us the strength to persevere through any trouble that comes our way today and protect us from any problem we may encounter in the future. Bestow us with compassion to better understand each other, to love and take care of each other, and give us harmony to live peacefully together.

When I go to bed, please, assist me in falling asleep serenely by helping me to remember that your compassion and mercy are new every morning.

Please, always remind me to count all my blessings and not taking them for granted. Help me be grateful and celebrate life. Right here. Right now.

Please, assist me when I am in physical pain. Ease my distress and guide me to whatever (rest, spiritual tips, medicines, alternative therapies, diet, ...) may immediately restore me to complete well-being.

Success and failure, pleasure and despair, ups and downs, whatever life brings to me, please, help me be powerful and free. Help me face adversity with a smile. Grant me the strength to remain happy despite any hardship and to enjoy life regardless of any circumstance.

Please, help me spiritually grow more and more to be like you. Please, make me a pure channel of divine love and guide me to places where I can be a blessing.

You know me deeply, truly as I am. You know that I have been addicted to sorrow and struggle for too long. Now, please, help me release this old addiction to unhappiness. Guide me to always choose light instead of darkness, strength instead of weakness, faith instead of doubt, and joy instead of suffering.

Whatever I have done, please give me the strength, courage and wisdom to forgive myself. Give me guidance so that I forgive myself and anyone else. Now and forever.

Please, keep me always on the path that leads to enlightenment and assist me in fulfilling my sole purpose. Ignite me with your power, shower me with joy and happiness, and make me ready for whatever wonder my soul has in store.

Please, help me heal any emotional wound that affects my relationships. Give me guidance to balance all dysfunctional relationships in my life with harmony, grace and emotional maturity.

Please, connect me with my soul's truth and spiritual power. Guide me into the depths of who I am on a soul level so that I may know and express my authentic self in life, relationships, business, and at every level of my being.

When I feel powerless, when I feel hopeless, when I feel weak, please, remind me that even with a little faith, as small as a mustard seed, I can move mountains.

Please, infuse my heart with divine peace. Clear it from all worries and anxieties, and make space for calmness. Please, make me feel at peace with myself and with the entire world.

Please, help me understand the lessons and not lose the blessings that come from every experience. Inspire me to continue to grow in awareness, love and light.

Thank you for uplifting me every day. I am grateful for knowing that you are always with me comforting my heart and whispering words of loving encouragement. Please, continue to surround me with your protection and love, and never cease to guide me to walk through life with your grace and mercy.

Please, inspire me to love at a wider and higher level. Empower me to bring love to every aspect of my life. Teach me how to fortify the foundation of love within myself so that I may become an unshakeable beacon of love for myself and everyone around me.

Please, infuse me with the fire of transformation and help me burn my ego's resistances. Give me the willingness to constantly move towards growth, renewal, happiness and positivity.

Please, fill me with the same kind of deep compassion towards all living beings that you carry within your angelic heart.

Please, make me an instrument of divine love. Enlighten my mind, open my heart, expand my awareness and strengthen my will so that I may become a human angel: a bearer of light and a messenger of love.

Please, help me let go of anything that is holding me back and open up to whatever the future has in store for me.

Please, help me forgive myself for all the times I have disappointed those who love me, those I wearied and harmed. Teach me not to hurt anyone, especially those who love me. Infuse me with your kindness, selflessness and generosity in love.

Thank you for assisting me with such patient loyalty, when I keep repeating similar life experiences over and over again without learning the lesson. Thank you for steadily assisting me as a caring teacher does with a stubborn kid.

Please, help me remove the resistances within me to freely express my sexuality. Infuse these resistances with the light of awareness so that I may become a channel of free, pure, unbounded and creative sexual energy. Help me explore, expand and enjoy my sexuality.

Please, make me aware that the past is behind me and the freedom to choose my future is ahead of me. Infuse me with the peace of knowing that I am right where I need to be, on the path to a wonderful tomorrow.

Please, help me to handle every difficult situation and every unexpected event with calmness, confidence and self-control. Infuse me serenity with your gentle whispers from above. Let me feel your loving presence so that I may calm my spirit.

Please, give me guidance to become aware of the emotional imbalances I have developed in this life and also of those I have inherited as a karmic legacy. Bring these emotional imbalances to my attention so that I may wisely work on them in order to move on and let go of anything that is binding my spirit.

Please, help me be content with little and satisfied with less. Guide me to find joy and pleasure in the simple things of life. Help me always remember that the simplest things bring the greatest delight.

Please, guide me to meet uplifting and inspiring people to share my life journey with. Send me like-minded friends for mutual support. Guide me to become the loving and cheering friend for them that I would wish for myself.

Please, give me the courage to always do whatever needs to be done. When I stall or doubt, please, lovingly kick me into action.

Please, heal my past. Release the painful memories and the traumas of old injuries from my mind, heart and physical body. Remove the pain of my past and erase the consequences of the poor decisions I made as a result of my brokenness. Show me how to find freedom from my emotional pain and enjoy the abundant life that God wants for me.

Please, infuse me with your angelic light. Shower me with your heavenly energy so that my blessings may be as abundant as the stars in the night.

When I feel impatient, please, bring me acceptance and inner peace. Remind me that God has perfect timing: never early, never late. Please, help me stop trying to move ahead of Him. Help me trust God's plan and always be mindful that I am exactly where I am meant to be.

Before taking any decision, please guide me to evaluate its consequences, the positive and the undesired ones. Infuse me with the wisdom to take judicious decisions in a very conscious way. Guide me to master my decision making, learn from the outcome of every decision and take full responsibility for it.

Please, help me to practice the art of patience by remembering that everything that I need or desire will be given to me in divine perfect timing.

Please, help me have faith, help me love, and help me remember that with love and faith I can make everything possible.

Please, guide me to understand the timeless mystery of life. Help me unveil the unfathomable reality that is hidden from everyday sight. Harmonize me with the power of Creation. Give answer to my quest for finding ultimate truth, inner peace and oneness with the Divine.

Please, give me guidance to transform my heart and mind so that I can learn to care and share. Help me be a gentle and loving presence in the world.

Please, give me guidance to strengthen my heart and inspire me to share words of wisdom where they are needed in the most respectful and careful way. Help me be a gentle and loving presence and leave this world better than I found it.

When I feel lost in the midst of the darkness, please help me not lose sight of your beam of light and faithfully follow it.

Please, infuse me with your light so that I may clear all the energy frequencies that are not aligned with love and compassion. Help me stay centred and wholeheartedly involved in my personal awakening process as I discover my purpose, mission and role on earth.

Please, help me be aware that my life is too precious to be wasted on doing things that I do not enjoy. Help me focus on what makes me the most happy. Inspire me to live a life true to myself with no sense of lack or regrets. Infuse me with the courage to follow my heart and pursue my passions.

Please, make easier and faster than ever before to connect with you. Assist me in understanding your heavenly guidance as I travel through life. Help me hear your words and put them into practice.

Please, help me remember that when I want to change something in my life, I must change from within and everything will spontaneously fall into place.

Please, help me be aware of how and where I am focusing my energy. Guide me to administer my energy properly. Allow me to only give my energy to the thoughts, words and deeds that effortlessly project me to the life of my dreams.

Please, help me release any judgment I make of others. Open me up to unconditional love, compassion and understanding. Help me unconditionally accept everyone as they are, with their personality, their hopes and dreams, their unique ways of being.

Please, keep my loved ones under the shield of your caring protection. Let them feel the blessing of your love as it pours through you. Please, shine your light brightly for them so that their hearts may always be unburdened of any weight.

I don't know who will cross my path today and what will happen, but I do know that you will watch over me to grant me protection in all situations. Thank you for caring and shielding me, allowing only positivity and love. Thank you for making me always feel safe and loved, today and every day of my life.

Please, guide me to be compassionate towards others and inspire me to always find the right way to comfort and cheer them up. Empower my voice so that I may be able to bring solace to their hearts and nourish their souls with uplifting words of wisdom.

Please, inspire me to always do the right thing. Make my heart brave and infuse me with courage so that I make the right decision in every circumstance, no matter how difficult or uncomfortable it might be.

Thank you for all your wonderful answers to my prayers. Thank you for helping me in my hour of need. Thank you for the big and little miracles that you make possible every day. I thank God immensely for the blessing of having you in my life.

Please, help me not seek peace and happiness outside of myself. Guide me to seek them where they have always been, in the sacred place within my heart.

Please, instruct me about self-love. Guide me to love what I am and express this love in a way that generously flows from my heart with joy and gratitude. Inspire me to build caring relationships with others from this place of self-love.

When I am tempted to give up, please help me not to be discouraged. Help me to be confident, cheerful and completely trust into my happy ending.

Please, guide me to be a beacon of light for all I encounter. Give me guidance to always find uplifting words when they most need to hear them. Inspire me to speak to their hearts so that they may remember their magnificence and be encouraged to shine their own brilliant light.

Please, give me the clarity to avoid things that can potentially harm me. Guide me to be attentive and mindful so that I may choose only what is good for me and all concerned.

Please, help me lift my heart above my problems and heaviness. Give me your clear guidance so that I may unveil the lesson and the blessing that every difficult situation brings.

Please, give me guidance so that I may remove any block in my mind and heal any emotional wound that could make me afraid of love. Help me take the risk of opening my heart up to love.

Thank you for your unconditional love for me. Help me extend that same love, mercy, care and protection to all.

Please, help me be a channel of divine healing. When someone is suffering, let my love flow and naturally find its way to their hearts. Inspire my words and actions so that I may be the embodiment of divine love.

Please, remind me to always include the happiness of others in the pursuit of my own.

Please, help me mirror your love to others. Help me be like you so that I may bless and enlighten the lives of all I touch.

Please, show me how to understand you more clearly. Make your messages so explicit that your precious advice may become unmistakable to me. Please, connect with me in ways that I can effortlessly comprehend so that I may receive clear and perfect guidance and fully benefit from your loving support.

Please, help me go through this day inspired by your goodness, knowing that your gentle hand steers my course and leads me to walk the straight and narrow.

Please, help me heal and be free from the negative effects of anger, resentment and thoughts of revenge. Soothe my soul and guide me to find a way to just let go and lovingly embrace forgiveness.

Please, protect and help all my loved ones. Grant them peace and happiness. Watch over them and keep them safe in all they do and wherever they go. Spread your mighty wings over them and encompass them in your circle of heavenly love.

Please, calm my emotions and mind, so that I may discern the precious guidance you offer me. Make stronger and clearer the intuitive thoughts I receive from you so that I may fully profit from your blissful assistance and wise advice.

Please, give me the firmness not to allow anyone to verbally or emotionally abuse me. Give me the boldness not to tolerate mistreatment from anyone. Teach me the deep meaning of self-respect so that the way I treat myself may become the way I allow others to treat me.

Every morning when I wake up, please fill my heart with the joy of being alive and inspire me to go through my day with my heart overflowing with bliss and gratitude. Help me focus on what I have, and have a deep and genuine appreciation for this incredible experience called life.

Please, infuse me with the vision of a peaceful future for humanity and give me the will to constantly work to make this vision real. Awaken me to the ultimate truth, the oneness of life, and make me a divine tool of this truth to bring humanity into the golden age of brotherhood, prosperity and enlightenment.

Please, provide me with loving friends to share my deepest feelings. Send my way true friends who accept me for who I am without judging or trying to change me. Please, surround me with people who do not deny my humanity but unconditionally embrace it.

When certain thoughts, which counter my true desire and happiness, pass through my mind please help me not to feed or strengthen them. Help me not to give them power or be their neutral beholder so that they may disappear as quickly as they came to the surface of my silent mind.

Please, let the words of my mouth speak the truth with humbleness and simplicity so that everyone may understand and benefit from them.

When I am worried, please, guide me not to see the situation as a problem. Help me recognize it as a divine opening and unexpected pathway into receiving all I deserve and wish for.

Please, guide me to create relationships with my family and friends based on respect and trust so that I no longer have the need to tell them how to be and what to do. Guide me to lovingly support their own choices and respect their free will.

Please, hold my hand in weakness and shower me with strength when I waver in faith. Infuse me with the serenity to always remember that I am never alone, because you are with me through the most challenging moments of my life, helping to carry my burdens, instructing me when I err in judgment and encouraging me when I am disheartened.

Please, make me ready to seize my greatness. Give me the mindsets and skill sets that allow me to remove any limiting belief that prevents me from setting powerful goals and achieving my dreams.

When I am offended or disappointed by someone, please help me not allow the hurt dwell in my heart. Help me let no resentment and bitterness take root in it. Take away all anger in me and embrace in your perfect, divine peace.

Please, help me return my physical, emotional and spiritual bodies to wholeness and balance. I ask for your angelic divine healing at all levels of my being.

Please, give me guidance so that I may remove whatever bitterness there is in my heart, and fill the empty spaces with love and bliss.

I ask you to shelter and protect me from any negative energy. Please, wrap me with your wings as an inviolable shield of light. Let me rest in your embrace so that I may regain the confidence and the strength to keep all negative, low and dark energies away.

Please, help me feel the oneness of everything in my heart so that I may be at one with all that is.

Please, fill every moment of my life with enthusiasm, passion and childlike curiosity. Every day infuse me with the excitement of a fresh start. Restore my true essence so that I may become pure and innocent as a newborn child with not a care in the world, and so much to learn and wonder.

Please, help me forgive myself for letting my hurt take control over me and for wounding others because of my wounds.

Please, infuse inner strength in me and give me the power and the bravery to do what it takes to overcome any obstacle that stands in the way of my dreams.

Please, touch my mind and give me your loving thoughts. Touch my heart and give me your infinite compassion. Touch my lips and give me the ability to speak your words. Touch my body and transmit your willingness to act and your talent to do well in this world.

Please, let me hold your hand and walk like a child by your side, confident in your ever-present protection, fortitude and love.

Please, help me love like you love, in a heavenly and all-embracing way. Help me never seek vengeance and embrace with mercy and love everyone, even my enemies and those who harm me.

Please, teach me how to connect with the infinite source of light within my heart. Help me let my light shine and spread throughout the world. Inspire me to be the mirror for others to radiate their own sparkling light.

Please, strengthen my connection to the Divine. Help me walk my life path with the highest energy and experience love in its highest form. Show me how to rise above any lower energy and keep my vibration high throughout the day.

Please, help me let go of control and remember that I cannot plan my future. Help me always remember that the universe has a plan for me and my job isn't to be in control of it: it's just to trust and go along with it.

Please, fill my heart with childlike joy today and every new day of my life. Guide me not to lose this fascination with the wonders of life. Inspire me to preserve the excitement for what comes next and always see the tomorrow as the bearer of endless possibilities.

I ask for your divine protection from negativity so that it may not affect my energy field in any way and for any reason. Please, help me be centered in love and allow no negativity to enter my space and interfere or diminish the fullest expression of my joyful soul essence.

Please, help me let go of any self-judgement created by my ego to keep me small. Infuse me with self-confidence so that I have nothing to fear about my greatness. Guide me to unleash the greatness inside me and unlock the power to break through any limit so that I may create the life I desire.

Please, guide me to never confuse the pursuit of material wealth with the search of material power. Help me not give way to the seduction of material power in any form used to tempt and flatter me.

Please, help me set peace as a deep intention and no longer be in conflict with myself. Guide me to find peace within so that I may carry it forward into my daily life. Help my peace be contagious and make a positive impact on other people's lives.

Please, inspire me to enjoy the simple beauty of silence. Help me practise inner silence so that I may boost the clarity of my mind. Remind me that a few minutes of inner silence every day can change my life in a way that I cannot even imagine.

I ask for your guidance in my decisions. Please, help me be generous and not make selfish decisions for my comfort, the approval of others, or for fear of their disapproval.

Please, ignite the flame of the spiritual quest within me; infuse me with a restless desire for truth. Lead me towards enlightenment and help me avoid the pitfalls I may find along the way, as the road is glorious but difficult to climb. Help me continue faithfully on my path, even when it seems to lead nowhere, and proceed steadily until I reach my goal.

Please, shelter me under your wings and keep me away from negative energies. Protect me from dark shadows, negative forces and hostile entities from the unseen world. Encompass me in your blessing and protection. May your wings be a barrier that surrounds me so that I may always feel safe and out of danger in your mighty arms.

Please, let my light glow unconcerned of the darkness around me; guide my spirit to rise above all the difficulties, challenges, problems and obstacles I may find along the path. Allow the stream of life to expand my heart to a deeper level of consciousness until I reach my highest potential of goodwill, grace and love.

Please, guide me to be righteous, courageous and audacious. Guide me to always do what is right and not what is easy. Guide me to choose what challenges me and not what makes me feel comfortable.

Please, help me strengthen my connection to mother earth. Inspire me to always act as her caretaker and to respect, protect and honor all the life forms that reside on her.

Please, guide me to trust in the power and wisdom of love in such a natural way as I trust in the air I breathe.

Please, grant me to open my heart to the loving kindness of my spirit and soul. Give me guidance so that I may know, love and express my own angelic self.

Please, guide me to treat everyone as the divine beings that they are. Guide me to treat myself as the divine being that I am.

Please, help me heal my emotional wounds. Infuse me with the courage to dive into the source of my tears and into the depths of my fears to bring the light of awareness and re-emerge purified by love.

Please, remind me what my soul has known forever. Help me remember that my inner light has always been there, and will always be there. Make me ready to embrace the light within and allow it to shine brightly in the world.

Please, help me not drop to low frequencies, based on patterns and habits ruled by my old emotional wounds. Help me constantly hold the highest energies in my heart so that I may always be aligned with the frequencies of heaven on earth. Make me ready to embody infinite love and be prepared for the incoming frequencies of the new earth.

To your guidance and love, I surrender my problems. I surrender them knowing that they will be completely solved through you in the most loving and merciful way for myself and all concerned. I surrender my worries to you knowing that, thanks to you, peace will be restored within my mind and heart.

Please, help me no longer allow my past fears to control my present and my future. Guide me to live every moment light-heartedly, free from all and any conditioning, burden, trouble and worry of the past.

Every time I identify myself with my personal dramas, please, help me look beyond them. Always remind me that they are part of my growing process. Enlivened, glowing and whole, make me ready to learn how to grow through adversity.

Please, guide me to align my life experience to my soul purpose. Heal my heart of any wound that may interfere with my fulfillment. Give me guidance to look into myself to embrace my divine purpose and find out what makes my soul sing.

Please, guide me to always tell the truth even when it is so hard to do it. Inspire me to communicate difficult truth with love, care and sensitivity.

Please, help me cultivate an intimate relationship of connection with you, communicating with you, opening my heart to you, relying on you and trusting you.

Please, sow the seeds of unconditional love within my heart. Open my eyes to see the good in other people and never let me be blinded by prejudice. Inspire me to see everyone with the compassionate eyes of love.

When I am upset with someone, please, help me remember that everyone is a child of Love. Calm me down so that I may replace the wish for revenge with understanding, and anger with compassion.

Please, help me focus on what I love and what fills my heart with passion. Help me remove myself from situations and relationships that dampen my fire. Ignite my spirit and allow me to fully connect with my inner power and my inner divinity.

Please, guide me not to hurt anyone, consciously or unconsciously, with my words and deeds. Help me be more attentive toward others and to move through life with sensitivity, respect, humbleness and grace.

When I fail, please help me not give up or see myself as a victim of misfortune. Give me guidance so that I may persist and be able to see the failure as a life lesson that leads me on the path I was meant to walk. Help me allow myself to embrace my defeat and unveil the glory concealed in the lesson I have learned.

When the power of hope is lacking in my life and I feel crushed, please, let me rest in your embrace so that I may regain the confidence and the courage to go on stronger than before. Hold me within your compassionate embrace and give me the strength not to allow anything or anyone, for any reason whatsoever, to put me down.

Please, watch over me and my loved ones and cover us with your shield of protection. Surround us with your beautiful and powerful healing light and assist us in all we do. Provide us a safe haven in your arms. Now and forever.

Please, give me the wisdom not to be ashamed of my weakness. Help me accept and show myself for what I am. Teach me the right mindset so that what once was my weakness may become my power and my strength.

Please, teach me how to practise unconditional love. Guide me to stop judging and allow everything to be as it truly is. Let my love flow free, all-encompassing, boundless, and unreserved. Empower me to love everyone wholeheartedly and work for the good of everyone with no expectations.

Please, help me stay focused and not be too easily distracted by things that might take me away from my path of self-realisation. Guide me to never divert my attention away from what brings me peace, harmony and joy.

Please, neutralize every evil intent to harm me or any member of my family. Protect all of us with your bright shield of light so the power of those who intend to harm us will instantly melt away like snow in the sun.

When I feel fear, please hold my hand. Remind me that under your mighty shield of light there is nothing to worry about, nothing to be afraid of. Infuse me with confidence, courage and power so that I may be stronger than any worry and fear in my life.

Please, every day remind me to honor the sacredness of life in everything and everywhere. Every day, give me guidance so that I may move forward on my sacred journey of discovery and growth.

Please, guide me to work for the greater good. Inspire me to give kindness and care wherever needed. Inspire me to do what needs to be done for the benefit of all mankind. Provide me all the spiritual tools to change my life forever, and to live and act for a purpose greater than myself.

Please, help me be aware of and accept my limits but never believe that they are unbeatable. Shower me with the courage to move beyond them so that I may manifest my unlimited and highest potential.

Please, guide me to replace my old limiting beliefs about money with new, positive thoughts. Guide me to benefit from the abundance that the Universe provides so that I may experience an existence of blissful and unlimited prosperity.

Please, protect me and prevent other people's low vibrations from affecting me. Shield me so that I may not absorb any toxic energy around me coming from distressed or angry people. Give me guidance to keep my vibration high and communicate to everyone the peaceful energy of love.

Please, remind me to respect boundaries and not to impose my help on anyone. Give me acceptance so that I may not feel frustrated when someone refuses my assistance. Help me remember that everyone has their own path to walk, their own challenges to face and their own life to live.

Please, help me release all my old programming of limitation and privation, and allow the natural abundance of everything in the universe to freely flow into my life.

Please, make me aware that I am always surrounded by your grace and make my heart overflow with gratitude. Remind me that I am immensely loved and supported by you and by entire legions of Angels.

Please, give me guidance to stop waiting for something outside of myself to make me happy. Teach me how to tap into the infinite, inexhaustible and ever present, source of happiness that dwells within myself.

When I become prey to my low-frequency emotions, please, remind me not to identify with them. Remind me that I am not my anger, my worries, my fears and my attachments. Remind me that I am my highest potential: I am bliss, love and compassion.

Please, help me stop expressing dissatisfaction with situations and people by criticizing, grumbling and finding all that is wrong. Help me stop complaining or give power to my personal dramas. Let me become the person who is pleasant and easy to be around. Guide me to radiate positivity and make the people around me feel relaxed, comfortable, peaceful and appreciated.

Please, guide me to focus on the good and the blessings that I constantly receive. Let me remain in a place of thankfulness, count my blessings, notice simple pleasures and acknowledge everything I receive. Make me aware that each and every day I have so much to be grateful for. Fill my heart with thanks and praise for a life that is extraordinary and beyond any imagination.

Please, help me get away from the noise of the world and be still so that I may give myself time and space to listen to your gentle whispers. Help me connect to your heavenly guidance and never miss a word of your precious promptings.

When I feel alone, please, remind me that loneliness is just an illusion because I have you always by my side. Remind me that I am always supported, guided, protected knowing you walk with me every step of the way.

Please, give me guidance so that I may stop comparing myself to others and seeing myself as inferior or superior to them. Help me see myself as a unique expression of the one life with the same value for life. Assist me in acknowledging that my talents and gifts are entirely unique as unique is my purpose in this world.

Please, help me not deny or repress my sensitivity and not label myself as weak because of it. Give me guidance so that I may recognize and accept it as a gift that brings me the ability to empathize and the blessing of a compassionate nature.

Please, make me able to protect myself from unwanted situations. Give me the discernment to say "Yes" only if "Yes" is my honest answer and not because I am driven by the fear to say "No". Remind me that putting myself first doesn't mean that I let others down. Give me guidance so that I may be always nice, kind, respectful and generous but never submissive.

Please, help me always remember to turn to you in prayer. Always remind me that prayer is the cure for a disordered mind, the remedy for a discouraged soul and the antidote for a poisoned heart.

When I experience anger, please, help me not lose my temper. Drive me into a peaceful place within myself where mercy and forgiveness reign.

Please, help me not to allow worries and bitterness dominate and define my life. Connect me with the never-ending flow of love and vibrant joy within me so that I may wholeheartedly embrace life and enjoy it with a divine sense of humour.

Please, guide me to detach myself from the role I am playing in life, from my problems, challenges and dramas. Awaken me to my inner power and the effortless freedom of my divine nature.

Please, silence my mind. Help me breathe the silence and listen to my heart so that I may remember that everything is love and I am that love.

Please, inspire me to be love in action, ready to unconditionally help and support others. Help me love and help others without conditions or expectations so that I may express my angelic nature. Open up my life to the beauty, wisdom, good will and delight of my angelic essence.

Please, help me release any judgment and criticism of others. Help me give space to them to be who they are, so that I can, in turn, be myself.

Before doing anything, please, make my intentions clear so that everything happens as a perfect result of my clear intentions.

Please, help me release delusional beliefs and depressive thoughts about myself or the world. Guide me to overcome the mind pattern of being a worrier and make me a believer.

Please, take my hand and guide me away from my emotional scars into the light of fearless love. I ask for your healing in my wounded parts so that the clouds in my heart may lift, and I may feel love, radiate love, be love.

Please, help me release all patterns within my mind that generate illness and disease. Clear the old belief systems that no longer serve me. Disconnect the energies of the past so that I may effortlessly let go of everything that is holding me back and start to create a brand new amazing life.

Please, give me guidance to find the strength to be gentle, the humbleness to forgive, the willingness to be understanding, and the openness to love and be loved in return.

Please, teach me how to love my foes, how to bless those who curse me, how to be merciful to those who despise me, how to pray for those who mistreat me and how to forgive those who hurt me. Help me be compassionate, radiant and blissful as you.

Thank you for clearing away my insecurity and fear, and showing me that I am a spark of divine light here to enlighten this world, be happy and give joy to everyone who crosses my path.

When things don't work out the way they're supposed to, please, inspire me to practise acceptance, be faithful and trust into your powerful help to provide everything I need for my challenging and unique journey here on earth.

Please, help me always remember that I am one with life and every human being is an expression of the divine and sacred life. Give me a compassionate understanding for all paths since all paths are one.

Please, help me not miss any personal or professional chance because of my need for security. Infuse me with the strength and bravery necessary to challenge myself and be amazingly successful.

When I feel needing love, please remind me that lack of love is just an illusion. Remind me that I am loved beyond measure and blessed beyond words.

Please, support me in granting myself the freedom to be who I am in the present moment. Give me the self-confidence not to try to conform myself to social patterns derived from ideas that others have about the "right" way to live. Help me truly live my life and not just merely exist.

Please, set me free from the shackles of unhappiness. Settle me back into a sense of positivity and confidence. Help me relax, be trusting, stop chasing happiness and let happiness find me.

Please, remind me that I am capable of achieving anything I put my focus on, will or mind to. Remind me that I am stronger and braver than I believe. Help me stand in my power confidently.

Please, heal every hidden part of myself that is still unconsciously wielding its obscure power over my life. Give me guidance so that all that has been hidden will be illuminated by the bright light of consciousness.

Please, assist me in reaching my life goals with ease and successfully. Give me your guidance to achieve my potential so that I may make every plan that I have borne in my heart succeed.

Please, give me the wisdom to always draw from the sacred source of my heart, loving the whole world as a reflection of the unconditional love I feel for myself.

Every time you whisper your gentle advice to me, please, help me recognize and trust your voice. Help me burn away my ego and false pride so that I may be open and willing to follow your divine guidance.

Please, make me able to forget all harm received. I ask you to totally fill my heart with forgiveness and compassion so that there is no room left for anger and resentment.

When my heart is cast down at seeing no results come from my endeavors, please, grant me a hopeful spirit. Offer me the confidence I need to go forth so that I may see the miracles that arise from believing and trusting.

Please, enlighten my way so that I may walk my life path with the guide of your glowing light and every step I take may be one step closer to the fulfillment of my soul contract on this earthly plain.

Please, awaken my heart to love so that I may open it, like a flower opens up to the warm rays of the sun.

Thank you, thank you immensely for your unconditional love. I know that whatever I have done and whatever others might think about what I have done, I am always your cherished child of love and light.

Please, guide me not to go through life on autopilot. Inspire me not to wearily spend each day just like the one before. Help me not to be a creature of habit and routine. Guide me to live fully, savour every moment and enjoy the ride with all its fantastic thrills.

Please, help me treat each person I encounter as I would like to be treated. Help me open up my eyes, mind and heart, to be attentive and sensitive to others so that every day I may find new, unexpected ways to practice acts of loving kindness.

Even when the truth might make me uncomfortable, even when it might make me suffer, please infuse me with the strength, resoluteness, persistence and honesty to always seek it.

Please, help me clear my mind from all negative thoughts, desires and beliefs that limit my complete and full potential.

I ask for your help to stop punishing myself for the mistakes I have made. Please, remind me that the greatest lessons I have learned in life come from my mistakes. Guide me to overcome every mistake I have ever made with the healing power of self-forgiveness.

Please, help me be kind, compassionate and inspire others. Fill me with loving goodness so that my thoughts, words, and actions may make a positive difference in this world.

Please, strengthen my spirit so that I can be able to encourage and support the souls of those who cross my path in life. Inspire me to share uplifting messages with them. Give me the power to bestow words of wisdom on those who need a loving guidance. Give me the power to give faith, hope and trust to those who are lost.

Please, give me guidance to make those around me feel loved. Help me be openhearted so that I may always show them how much they matter to me. Help me be mindful so that I may always acknowledge their love and never take it for granted. Make me able to show my recognition and gratitude abundantly for having them in my life.

Please, infuse inner strength in me and give me the power to do what it takes to overcome any obstacle that stands in the way of my dreams. Help me experience all that my heart desires with love and gratitude.

Please, guide me to be righteous, kind and compassionate so that I may set an example that others can follow.

I ask for your assistance to let go of what no longer serves my higher purpose. Please, give me the wisdom to close the doors that need to be shut and open the doors that need to be opened. Give me guidance so that I may let go of something old every day and learn something new every day.

Please, help me not cause others to suffer because of my selfishness. Widen my perspective from being self-focused to being open to all. Give me guidance so that I may walk in your footsteps and generously bestow love and goodness.

Please, help me go straight on when life tries to derail my plans. Correct me when I go astray. With your loving touch, keep me always on track so that I may proceed with positivity and effortlessness in the direction of my greater good.

Please, be with me through the most challenging moments of my life. Infuse me with the strength to stand strong in adversities. Remind me that it is what I have learned from the challenges I faced that have led me to be where I am now on my sacred path in life.

Please, clear my mind from any image of unhappiness, guilt, abandonment, loneliness or lack of love. Guide me to bring my focus back to the present and break the repetitive cycles derived from the emotional wounds of my childhood. Reset these cycles, align me with positivity so that I may consciously change my "default" programming into a new awesome one, based on happiness, self-realization and abundance of everything.

Please, help me cleanse traumatic memories stored in my body and at any level of my being. Help me release stress, pain, fears and any energy block that prevent my energy to flow freely. Give me guidance so that I may release any unhealthy emotional pattern and replace it with love and freedom.

Please, instruct me about self-acceptance. Help me accept my body and its defects, my character and its weaknesses. Help me stop trying to change myself into another person and fully embrace who I am.

When I am overwhelmed by painful emotions, please, let me rest underneath your mighty wings of love and dwell within your blissful heart. When I am afraid of the future, please, remind me that I can always lean on you and we will walk through each moment, whatever happens, together.

Please, fill me with the determination to let go of all the relationships that lower my energies. Help me let them go with love and gratitude. Infuse me with the courage to cut the 'deadwood' in my life and prepare myself for new growth.

Please, never stop whispering to me "You are forgiven" until I ultimately release my need for atonement and forgive myself.

Please, assist me in making decisions effortlessly. Unveil the limiting beliefs that sabotage my efforts. Banish bad habits that hinder me from fulfilling my divine purpose. Clean up the mental clutter that is holding me back from creating the life of my dreams.

Please, give me the confidence to live my life according to the principle that anything is possible for those who believe. Remind me that I can create miracles by simply opening my heart to divine love and grace.

Please, take my hand and guide me out of the dark places within myself into the light of my divine nature. Remind me that, even in the most obscure moments of my life, I can be a blessing, a gift for someone. Remind me that my light always shines.

Bless me with a new sense of self-worth so that I may acknowledge my efforts and accept my defeats. Hold my hand in my moments of weakness and give me strength when I waver in faith. With you, I have no reason for concern and nothing to fear.

Please, assist me in releasing the fear of being rejected and losing love if I am emotionally honest. Give me the willingness to share my deepest feelings with those I love without fear of judgment. Help me be open so that I may experience the joy of sharing with a wide, expanded heart.

Please, help me release the belief that I am not good, not smart, not good-looking enough. Help me stop thinking "I can't do it" and start to think "Everything is possible for me. The universe is my accomplice in all my enterprises."

No matter if my environment is messy and confusing, no matter what happens 'out there', please, anchor me in the steady center of peace, compassion and love within myself.

Please, help me stay heart centred. Help me let go of control and expectations with myself. Let me confidently surrender to the flow of life and trust love to handle the details.

Please, give me guidance so that I may go forward even when I feel like giving up, smile even when I don't feel like it, love even when it hurts and forgive even when I can't forget.

Please, help me stop allowing my mind to be driven by selfish impulses. Teach me how to brush away my egoism, arrogance, conceit, greed and intolerance. Help me break down the walls around my heart. Guide me to leave behind a life of selfishness and embrace selflessness.

Please, remind me to honour and bless every step I take in my path of life, every moment in which I shared my happiness on the way. And remind me to always thank you for your loving guidance along this journey of discovery and magic.

When a relationship ends and someone chooses to leave my life, please, infuse me with a sense of acceptance. Help me let go, bless them and remember that what is happening is nothing but the result of the accomplishment of our soul contract.

Please, help me be careful with whom I spend my time and to avoid people who drain my energies. Help me surround myself only with those who encourage, inspire and uplift me.

Please, assist me so that I may stop focusing on readjusting and managing my life on the outside. Help me make meaningful shifts in consciousness. Guide me to change from within so that I may transform my life from the inside out.

Although my desire to help others is strong and mighty, please, make me aware that I cannot help anybody who doesn't want to be helped. Guide me not to feel responsible for the destiny of others since every soul chooses their life journey according to their free will. Help me not to interfere with their choices but rather bless their paths, pray for them and love them unconditionally.

Please, guide me to heal my problematic relationships. Bring my frequency into harmony with my partner's, friends' and family's so that we can grow together. Help me send love to the relationships in my life that need help and let the power of love work on them.

Please, teach me how to enjoy every minute of my life. Give me guidance, infuse me with confidence so that I may live my life to the fullest, and experience happiness and fulfillment at every breath.

Every day when I wake up, please help me greet the day with gratitude and a positive attitude. Help me focus my first thoughts of the day on the good that I have in my life. Remind me that I am immensely blessed and fill my heart with thankfulness for the gift of life. Make me feel complete, wealthy, satisfied and blessed.

Please, infuse me with deep understanding, true knowledge, higher perception of reality and a natural ability to change everything for the better.

Please, help me understand that I deserve to be loved not only by the people around me but by the most important person in my life: me. Help me let my self-love grow and blossom so that I may live a fulfilled and thriving life.

Please, give me guidance so that I may stop complaining about misfortune and take responsibility for my life and my happiness. Help me overcome my victim mentality and step into the power of my spiritual mastery.

Please, enrich my life, fuel my interests and expand my knowledge. Bless me with a passion for learning and an insatiable curiosity so that I will never cease to grow.

In the hardest of times, please, hold my hand tightly and walk with me. Strengthen my confidence and never let the light of hope fade in my heart. Help me go through the storm until I see the rainbow.

Please, guide me to release my feelings of guilt when I disappoint the expectations of those who would like me to be different. Teach me self-acceptance so that I may be confident in all I do, that I may no longer need the approval from others to allow myself to be myself.

Please, remind me that all is perfect in the world, as the Divine wants it to be. Always remind me that my life flows according to the divine purpose so that I can surrender myself, my worries, cares, problems and needs to the will of God.

Please, infuse me with joy and delight. Give me the desire to sing, dance and laugh. Help me stop feeling sad no matter what the reason so that I may feel happy no matter the reason.

Please, help me reconnect with my pure, sacred, joyful essence. Help me complete my healing journey and return to a state of natural happiness and joyous living. Give me your loving guidance so that I may bring out the divine child within.

When things in my life are about to change in an unforeseen way, please, help me accept them with a confident spirit and not try to hold on to what is being altered. Give me your guidance so that, instead of feeling the pain of the end, I may feel the joy of a new beginning.

Please, awaken the infinite capacity for love within me. Help me constantly hold the energy of love in my heart so that I may always walk the highest path and serve the highest good.

Please, help me be honest and bold. Give me guidance so that I may stop sweeping things under the rug or withholding truth because of my lack of courage. Please, infuse me with the bravery of truth-telling.

Please, burn away my false pride and grant me the grace to be humble. When I am tempted to give in to the flatteries of pride, please, keep me simple and humble in heart. Make me wise and not boastful or arrogant. Help me to humble myself and live an unselfish life of service to others.

Other books by Human Angels

Have a look at how many other inspiring books we have written for you

We Are Human Angels - A Crash Course for Angelic Humans

Find out why this book can really change your life.

There is a Human Angel within all of us just waiting to be set free!

If you feel you are a Human Angel, you will recognize yourself in this book. Here you can find all of the answers to the most profound questions about yourself and the meaning of your presence here on earth. Have you, since childhood, felt to be different from your peers? Have you always been gifted with an out of the ordinary sensitivity and can't stand injustices? Have you never been able to relate yourself to other people according to the painstaking rules of society? If your answer to one or all of these is yes, then this book is for you.

In this book, you will find the greatest treasure of the world, You. The True You. Through this book, you will unearth the Angelic Side within you and this revelation will thoroughly change your life. You will find acknowledgement and appreciation through others in virtue of those qualities. Those qualities that have made you feel different so far.

How much pain do you regularly see around you? How strong is your desire to help others? By reading this book, you will learn how to manage and put to use your intense sensitivity as a Human Angel in relationships with others. You will learn how to be truly helpful to others in respect to their own free will.

We are Human Angels is a global phenomenon marked by the uniqueness of its story. It is, in fact, a self-published book, which can only be purchased at online bookstores. Because of this, *We are Human Angels* has not been given the usual promotion and marketing efforts that normally the traditional publishing houses do with their newest releases.

Nevertheless, in a very short time after its publication, many readers from different nationalities, having read this book, have been deeply touched by the strength and profoundness of its words. These readers have started to contact the authors offering to translate this book into their own native languages. Through this book you will realize that what you have been carrying, all your life, as a heavy burden weighing on your shoulders were in reality your wings. The time has come for you to spread them and begin to fly.

We wish you a fantastic journey!

The authors.

About this book, some of the readers have said:

Barbara A.: *"I love this book - I read it over and over again so the beauty of each and every word can penetrate my heart -body and Soul - it is truly My Soul Food for the day - I do not know who wrote the words on the pages or who published the book and it does not matter - it has touched me - like no other - it has fed me like no other -it has inspired me like no other."*

Alden C.: *"I recommend this book to everyone, whether you think you're spiritual or not. And to those on the spiritual path, I recommend this to you whether you are a seasoned sage or a greenhorn in the path. Other books could be written to expound on the 7 keys to overcome the ego and the 7 keys to live with the heart. This is book is a jewel! To those gifted souls who wrote the book, a million thanks to you!"*

Marc B.: *"Wonderful book uplifts me every day, have been looking for God and have found Him in other beings around me."*

Edward S.: *"Excellent source of guidance to better understand one's existence on this earth!"*

We Are Human Angels, We Inspire Change
A Complete Course for Angelic Humans

After the worldwide success of the first edition, by popular demand, here comes the extended edition *We are Human Angels, We Inspire Change - A Complete Course for Angelic Humans.*

In the first book, you have discovered your divine nature and have started to put into practice what you have learned. If you have loved the first course, you might be interested in further expanding your consciousness. This is why we offer you *We are Human Angels, We Inspire Change - A Complete Course for Angelic Humans.*

The book has more than doubled in size; all the contents of the first edition have been put under a magnifying glass. *We are Human Angels, We Inspire Change* offers you a deep dive into every topic, including in-depth analysis and practical examples. It is a fully equipped wisdom package to give you more tools to change your life forever, and to make the world a better place. If you are a badass truth seeker, you cannot miss this book.

Here you will find a summary of the contents of the book.

In the first part of the book, you will be guided in finding out about the ego and its repetitive, painful patterns. Knowing how the ego works is the first step to getting rid of it, awakening the

Human Angel within you, and finally shining all the light of your Being.

Here you find a summary of the contents of the book.

1.1 The Oneness and the ego

The ego is the illusion of separation that makes you believe that on one side there is you and on the other side the rest of the world, when the truth is that we are all One. In this first chapter, you will realize that the Oneness is neither an abstract concept nor is it an ideal to be pursued. Oneness is what you truly are, even when you are unaware of it. You will learn how to miraculously transform your life through the awareness of the Oneness.

1.2 Judgment

Judgment is the matrix of the ego. Every time you judge either yourself or others, you separate yourself from the Oneness. In this chapter you will discover how to stop judging and how to open your heart to Unconditional Love, that is Love in absence of judgment.

1.3 Guilt

Do you know that you are the most implacable judge of yourself? Do you realize that by judging yourself you feed your own sense of guilt? Are you aware that your feelings of guilt prevent you from fully realizing yourself? In this chapter, you will learn how to feel free of guilt and how to give yourself permission to be happy.

1.4 Projections

Why are you always attracted to a particular type of partner? Why do you always end up creating the same kind of difficult romantic relationship? In the fourth chapter, you will discover how to break free from this vicious circle of dissatisfaction and suffering. You will find all of the keys to building a healthy and satisfying romantic relationship.

1.5 Forgiveness

Do you know that the emotional wounds of your past remain imprinted in your cellular memory and continue to produce more and more distress? In the fifth chapter, you will learn that you can heal old emotional wounds, by clearing your cellular memory through the power of forgiveness. You will also realize that there is no greater healing than the forgiveness of oneself.

1.6 Fear

Your fears are like powerful magnets that attract exactly what you fear into your life. In the sixth chapter, you will discover how to stop believing the illusion of fear and how to stop unconsciously creating what you do not really want to create: failure, suffering, conflicts, ... You will learn how to manifest only what you consciously choose to manifest.

1.7 Acceptance

By reading this chapter, you will discover how

to change starting from the acceptance of your life. By learning to confidently surrender to the flow of life, you will always find yourself exactly where you want to be.

The second part of this book helps you to recognize and to fully express your mission as a Human Angel.

2.1 The Rebirth

You will learn how to make sense of your suffering, to bless it and let it go. Now that you have completed your healing journey, the time has come to be reborn into the Oneness and to express what you really are: a Human Angel.

2.2 The Intelligence of the Heart

In this chapter, you will find out what the Intelligence of the Heart is and how to use it to consciously create your own reality. It is through the wisdom of the Intelligence of the Heart that Human Angels become love in action.

2.3 Integrity

This chapter will help you to harmonize the different planes of your existence (physical, emotional, mental, and spiritual) at a higher level, where the spiritual plane enlightens all the others. You will discover how to bring within reach all the energies that were previously dissipated in continuous inner conflicts and how to coalesce them to the full realization of yourself.

2.4 The Here and Now

You will be guided on a journey through the timeless time of the Oneness: the Here and Now, that is the Human Angels' time. By learning how to live in the Here and Now, you will also learn that, when the past ceases to affect the future, everything becomes possible for you, even miracles.

2.5 Free Will

How much pain do you constantly see around you? How strong is your desire to help others? By reading this chapter you will learn how to manage your intense sensitivity as a Human Angel and how to make the best use of it in helping others. You will learn how to be truly helpful to other people by respecting their own free will.

2.6 Silence

Do you know what the most powerful prayer of all is? It is Silence. In this chapter, you will discover how to contact the Divine within yourself through Silence. You will also learn how to tune in with the universal flow of love, joy, and abundance.

2.7 The Greater Good

The last chapter will help you to fulfill your highest potential as a Human Angel and to find your own mission here on earth. You will see the vision of a new life and of a new world appear clearly before your eyes.

Your healing journey through the pages of this

book has finally been accomplished. Now you are ready to make a positive difference in this world. Now you are ready to Inspire Change.

365 Mantras for Today

Find your inner peace. Light up the world around you with the power of positive thoughts

Do you feel the powerful urge to change your life but you don't know how to do it? Start from within and the rest will spontaneously fall into place. When negative emotions and thoughts attract crappy things into your life, it's time to drag and drop into trash your old belief system made of:

Mind gremlins: *"My life is a mess."*

Negative mind chatter: *"I'll never get over this problem."*

Mental noise: *"I'm not smart/attractive/successful."*

The time has come to attract into your life all of the wonderful things you dream of and that you deserve.

"I succeed in everything I do."

"I am love."

"I dare to live my dreams."

"I give myself permission to be happy."

365 Mantras for today is the book that provides you with everything you need to effortlessly change your life. Some mantras will purify you. Some others will help you in raising your energies. You will free yourself from fears, feelings of guilt, anger, resentment, and expectations. You will achieve Self-confidence, Gratitude, Acceptance, Joy and Self-respect. Every moment in your daily life is the right time to connect yourself with the power of positivity! And there's no better time than now. Enlighten your life with the power of positivity!

By being positive, I attract positive things.
By radiating love, I attract love.
By being bright, I attract the light.

Yesterday I was, tomorrow I will be,
but only Here and Now I Am.

I recognize, trust and follow
the voice of my heart.

I release the belief
that I am not good enough,

*I am fully confident
in my abilities to succeed.*

*It does not matter
what emotional states
other people around me are in,
I keep quiet and radiate love.*

*I am aware
of the creative power of my thoughts.
Because of this,
I have only positive thoughts.*

*I recognize the signs
that life shows me.
I rely on the perfect guidance
of synchronicity.*

*I stop complaining
because I do not have
enough love in my life.
Now I can finally feel*

that Life is Love itself.

Judging others,
I give power to the mind.
Accepting others,
I give power to Love.

For more information on the Human Angels' books please visit our official website

wearehumanangels.com

For your daily dose of inspiration, Angelic wisdom and tips for life, visit our blog:

wearehumanangels.org

Join our 1M likes Facebook Page

We Are Human Angels

@WeAreHumanAngels777

Stay connected with other like-minded people on our Facebook Groups:

Connecting Human Angels and

Human Angels of the World

Want to stay in touch with us? Have questions? Contact us: earthangelshouse@gmail.com

About the Authors

Human Angels are the self-published authors of five inspiring books that have become in a very short time the benchmark for the human angels' community around the world. Their first title, *We Are Human Angels - A Crash Course for Angelic Humans,* was released in 2012 and suddenly became the first self-published book spontaneously translated by the readers into 14 different languages. Within a few years they have self-published four more books, including the Extended Edition of *We Are Human Angels (A Complete Course for Angelic Humans), 365 Mantras for Today, 365 Wisdom Pills,* and their newest release, *365 Prayers To The Angels - Get your prayers answered and fulfill all your dreams with the help of the Angels.* They also run the worldwide known Facebook page 'We Are Human Angels' that counts more than 1M likes.

The authors are neither gurus nor spiritual teachers. Their books are the result of their personal journey and reflect their inner healing. When, at a later stage of their lives they realised that they were born for a greater purpose and that time had come for them to express their true nature, they took the decision to quit their regular jobs to "incarnate" as authors and share their healing journey. With the help of powerful, channeled energies that have, increasingly, guided and enlightened their spiritual path they have transmuted their experiences into

Awareness and Love and put them into words for the benefit of all human beings. In Free Will they have chosen to stay anonymous. However, they have agreed to being interviewed by some spiritual magazines: OM Times Magazine - podcast, How to Connect with Angels - podcast, and they are the cover story of Spiritual Biz Magazine). and their latest interview for Inner Peace Masterclass hosted by Julie Cairnes.

Text revision: Jenny Perdoni

Cover design: robert_graphics@Fiverr.com

One More Thing

We are self-published authors and we self promote through our social network sites, through our books, and through the word of mouth of our readers. Being self-published authors means that our books are not supported by the usual promotional efforts that traditional publishing houses give to their titles and authors. Everything we do, we do ourselves. Everything we write, we write ourselves. There are no professional editors, proofreaders or publishing agents behind the human angels' project. It all comes from our hearts and from our souls.

We know that every single word is important, every single reader's opinion matters, every single positive thought can cause a cascade of positive actions.

If this book has touched your heart and opened your mind, please write a review on the store from which you have purchased the book.

The best way to make this book more visible to potential readers is by word of mouth of readers as well as good reviews. A review is a gift for us. The more the reviews, the greater the visibility of the book and the higher the number of people who will be interested in reading it. It might be your review that will sparkle someone else's interest in the book, helping them to finally recognize their true nature as a Human Angel.

1000 Thanks from us and from all those who will be inspired by your words!

Contents

Introduction 5
The 7 Golden Rules to make your prayers
work amazingly 7
365 Prayers to the Angels 15
Other books by Human Angels 199
We are Human Angels-A Crash Course
for Angelic Humans 200
We are Human Angels-We Inspire Change-
A Complete Course for Angelic Humans 203
365 Mantras for today 208
About the Authors 213
One More Thing 215

Made in United States
North Haven, CT
21 September 2023